making a difference

Caring for Yourself

Jillian Powell

WAYLAND

making a difference

Caring for Others
Caring for the Environment
Caring for Your Pets
Caring for Yourself

Editor: Sarah Doughty
Designer: Jean Wheeler

First published in 1997 by Wayland Publishers Ltd
61 Western Road, Hove, East Sussex BN3 1JD

British Library Cataloguing in Publication Data
Powell, Jillian
Caring for Yourself – (Making a Difference)
1. Self-esteem – Juvenile literature 2. Self-acceptance –
Juvenile literature
I. Title
155.2

ISBN 0 7502 1942 4

Typeset by Jean Wheeler, in England
Printed and bound by G. Canale & C.S.p.A., Turin

Picture acknowledgements
Chapel Studios 8 bottom (Zul Mukhida); Chris Fairclough 17, Life File 15 (Chris Jones);
Reflections 5 bottom, 6, 7 top, 19 (top), 20, 21 top, 28 bottom; Robert Harding 9, 11, 25; Sally
and Richard Greenhill 4, 8 (top), 19 bottom; Tony Stone Worldwide 5 top, 12, 14 (Joe
McBride), 21 bottom (Tessa Codrington), 22 top (Jo Browne/Mick Smee), bottom (Jon Riley),
28 top (Lawrence Migdale); Wayland Picture Library 7 bottom, 13 top, 16, 18 and 23 (all by
Angus Blackburn), 24, 26 (APM), 29 (APM); Zefa 10, 13 bottom, 27. Cover commissioned
photography by Angus Blackburn.

Contents

When you were a baby, you were fed and cared for all the time.

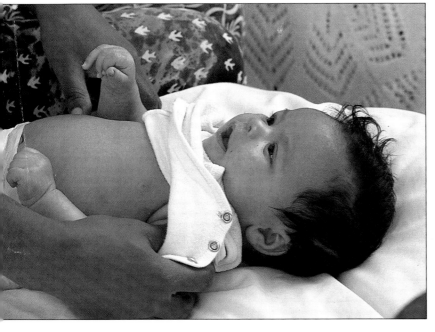

You were
given baths
to keep
you clean
and your
clothes were
changed.

Now you have learned to do more things yourself. A daily bath or shower keeps your body clean.

Try to eat lots of fresh fruit and vegetables but not too many cakes and sweets.

Exercise like running is fun and helps keep you fit and strong.

A crash helmet
helps to keep
you safe when
you are cycling
or skating.

Be aware of the heat of the sun. Wear suncream to stop it from burning your skin.

Wearing sunglasses takes care of your eyes. A sunhat helps to keep the sun off your head.

Keep yourself safe at home.
Electricity can be dangerous so let
a grown-up plug in the television for
your favourite programmes.

If you help in the kitchen, take care not to burn yourself on hot ovens, kettles or pans.

Stay safe when you are outdoors. Cross the road safely with a grown-up. Use a pelican or zebra crossing.

Never go to places by yourself. It is safer and more fun to go out with your family.

Only you know how you feel.

If you hurt yourself or don't feel well, tell someone about it.

You may need to rest or take some medicine to make you feel better.

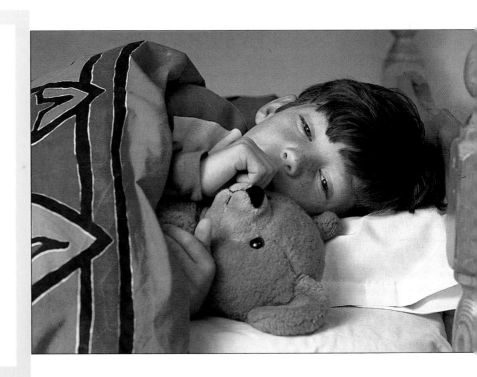

There are
people that
you like.
You want to
spend time
with them.

Our family and friends can make us feel happy.

If you feel sad or afraid, tell someone how you feel because talking can help.

Cuddle a toy or stroke a pet to
help yourself feel better.

Never let anyone make you do something that makes you feel unhappy or afraid.

If you are worried about anything, tell someone in your family or a good friend.

To be happy
and healthy,
work and
play hard
all day,
at school,
at home or
with friends.

You will feel your best during the day if you try and get plenty of rest and sleep at night.

Extension activities

MATHS

Survey your class to investigate favourite foods. Record your results in a graph form. From this can you decide if people eat healthily?

Measuring time using standard and non-standard units: How many jumps can you do in, for example, 30 seconds? With practice can you improve your times?

Count your pulse rate before and after exercise. Calculate the difference.

ENGLISH

Discuss emotional responses such as happiness and sadness. Encourage descriptive language. List words as shared writing.

Write a poem such as an acrostic using the word 'sadness'.

Look at the poetry of others to investigate how feelings have been interpreted.

MUSIC

Listen to classical pieces which evoke a range of moods.

Discuss the use of the music and sound effects on television to intensify suspense and fear.

Compose a range of sound effects to go with an emotional story.

HISTORY

Read biographies of people who have inspired other children, such as Helen Keller and Anne Frank.

Consider children's rights in the light of historical reform such as children working in factories, chimney climbers and so on. Use excerpts from novels such as *The Water Babies* to help illustrate those times.

SCIENCE

Consider safety in the kitchen or in the street. Draw a 'watch out!' picture to illustrate the dangers.

Discuss labelling on foods. Which foods have high sugar contents? What vitamins are included? What do the energy values mean and so on.

Use information books to investigate how the heart and lungs work. Investigate lung capacity.

Collect a selection of protective or special clothing such as gloves, hats or shoes. The children can make annotated drawings of each item to explain how they offer protection.

ART AND CRAFT

Make a collage from magazine cuttings to creatively portray healthy eating.

Discuss the use of reflective material for keeping safe during the dark evenings. Design an interesting logo made from reflective material to wear on coats.

DESIGN AND TECHNOLOGY

Discuss and make healthy and imaginative fillings for sandwiches. Children assess each one on merits of presentation, taste and nutrition.

Design and make a sun hat for themselves that is cool to wear and protects the eyes and neck.

P.E/DANCE/DRAMA

Focus on warming up different parts of the body before specific exercises. Discuss reasons for this with children. Relate to bones and muscles being used.

Devise a gymnastic sequence or dance that involves bending and stretching different parts of the body. Each group has a different focus.

Discuss setting personal goals and improving personal performance.

GEOGRAPHY

Discuss and list street furniture used to encourage safety. Make a survey of e.g. safe places to cross in the locality.

Draw four pictures to illustrate suitable clothing for each season.

R.E.

Read a variety of fables and stories such as *The Hare And The Tortoise, The Lion And The Mouse And Elmer*. Discuss the role of individual strengths and merits.

R.E.
- Fables and stories relating to individual strengths.

DESIGN AND TECHNOLOGY
- Sandwich fillings.
- Investigating protective clothing.
- Design and make a sunhat.

SCIENCE
- Safety in the street/kitchen.
- Investigating food labels.
- Using information books about the heart and lungs.
- Investigate lung capacity.

MATHS
- Surveying favourite foods.
- Making a block graph.
- Measuring time.
- Counting pulse etc.

HISTORY
- Biographies.
- Children's rights.

Caring for yourself
Topic web

ART AND CRAFT
- Collage.
- Designing a reflective logo.

ENGLISH
- Shared writing.
- Making lists.
- Composing poetry.
- Reading poetry.

GEOGRAPHY
- Surveying street furniture.
- Seasonal change.

P.E./DANCE/DRAMA
- Warming up activities.
- Gymnastic/dance sequence.
- Personal performance.

MUSIC
- Listening to classical music.
- Investigating moods.
- Composing sound effects.

Glossary

dangerous Something that can hurt you.

dentist Someone who looks after people's teeth.

electricity Power that moves along wires to make things work.

energy Strength in your body to do things.

medicine Special liquid or tablets that make you feel better when you are ill.

Books to read

How do I feel about...Looking after Myself? by Sarah Levete (Franklin Watts, 1996)

I Feel Sad by Brian Moses and Mike Gordon (Wayland, 1997)

Take Care on Your Own by Carole Wale (Wayland, 1996)

Who am I? by Jillian Powell (Wayland, 1993)

Index